A·M· BANKS

Constructing narratives

Book 1

Characters

- Drawing characters
- Describing characters
- Character passports
- Creating characters

Dialogue

- Effective dialogue
- Dialogue rules
- Designing dialogue
- Developing dialogue

Genres and settings

- Story genres
- Story settings
- Using the senses
- Creating a scene

Planning

- Story plans
- Making an ideas pack
- The story path
- Path of ideas

Drafting

- Beginning a story
- Continuing a story
- Ending a story
- Cover it

Revising

- Practising revising
- Revising the beginning
- Revising the middle
- Revising the end

Presenting

- Author profile
- Introducing you
- Story blurbs
- Introducing your story

Susie Brown

Published by Prim-Ed Publishing

0796C

CONSTRUCTING NARRATIVES
(Book 1)

Published by Prim-Ed Publishing 2006
Reprinted under licence by
Prim-Ed Publishing 2006
Copyright© Susie Brown 2005
ISBN 1 84654 032 1
PR–0796

Additional titles available in this series:
CONSTRUCTING NARRATIVES *(Book 2)*
CONSTRUCTING NARRATIVES *(Book 3)*

Offices in: United Kingdom: PO Box 2840, Coventry, CV6 5ZY   **Email:** sales@prim-ed.com
Australia: PO Box 332, Greenwood, Western Australia, 6924   **Email:** mail@ricgroup.com.au
Republic of Ireland: Bosheen, New Ross, Co. Wexford, Ireland   **Email:** sales@prim-ed.com
R.I.C. Asia: 5th Floor, Gotanda Mikado Building, 2–5–8 Hiratsuka,
Shinagawa-Ku Tokyo, Japan 142–0051   **Email:** elt@ricpublications.com

Internet websites

In some cases, websites or specific URLs may be recommended. While these are checked and rechecked at the time of publication, the publisher has no control over any subsequent changes which may be made to webpages. It is *strongly* recommended that the class teacher checks *all* URLs before allowing pupils to access them.

View all pages online

http://www.prim-ed.com

Foreword

Constructing narratives is a series of three books that have been designed to give pupils the skills to confidently write effective creative stories. The pupils are introduced to the writing process through activities that follow a step-by-step approach and progressively build upon the skills being learnt. Pupils plan, draft, revise and present creative stories that not only contain a beginning, middle and end, but have colourful characters, descriptive settings and effective dialogue.

Other titles in this series are:

- **Constructing narratives** Book 2
- **Constructing narratives** Book 3

Contents

Teachers notes

Constructing narratives is a series of three books designed to lead pupils through the process of creative writing. Each book is divided into seven sections that address different components of the writing process. These are:

- characters
- dialogue
- genres and settings
- planning
- drafting
- revising
- presenting

Each section contains four activities. The activities are accompanied by detailed teachers notes that provide examples and assessment checklists focusing on the skills being addressed. As each activity builds upon the skills learnt in the previous lesson, it is suggested that the worksheets be introduced in order, rather than at random. Each worksheet is designed to be completed in one lesson.

The structure of each book in the series is identical, with the activities having the same headings and main focus. This allows pupils with different ability levels to be working on the same activity in the one classroom. The activities increase in difficulty throughout the levels of the books. This allows for easy use within a multi-ability classroom.

Pupils will develop their understanding of the 'beginning', 'middle' and 'end' of a story and learn the requirements of each. Further activities allow pupils to focus on developing interesting characters, descriptive settings and dialogue that includes thoughts and actions.

Pupils will revise and polish their writing in stages—focusing on spelling and punctuation, correctly written dialogue and interesting text.

The activities lead pupils to create stories that have a plot and structure, as well as situations that are resolved by the final paragraph.

Note re punctuation: The punctuation used in this publication conforms to the rules set out in *Style manual for authors, editors and printers*, sixth edition, Wiley and Sons.

Teacher pages

Each pupil page is supported by a teachers page which provides the following information.

Objective(s) provides the focus of the lesson.

Teacher information provides suggestions for teaching the lesson. Specific examples and answers are included where appropriate.

Additional activities are suggestions to further develop the focus of the activity. They may also be used as extension activities for fast-finishing pupils.

The **Assessment checklist** provides a list of specific skills that should be demonstrated by the pupils. These can be used for either anecdotal or written assessment records.

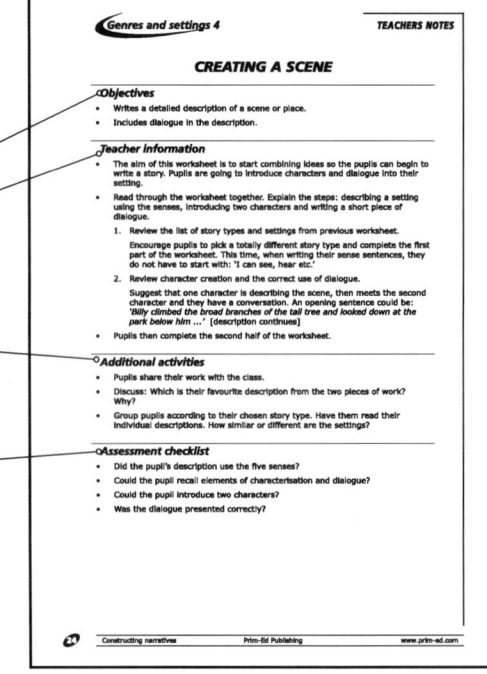

Pupil pages

Specific instructions are provided and space given for written responses.

Some worksheets allow for pupils to illustrate their ideas.

Where appropriate, handy hints and reminders are given to help pupils complete the activity.

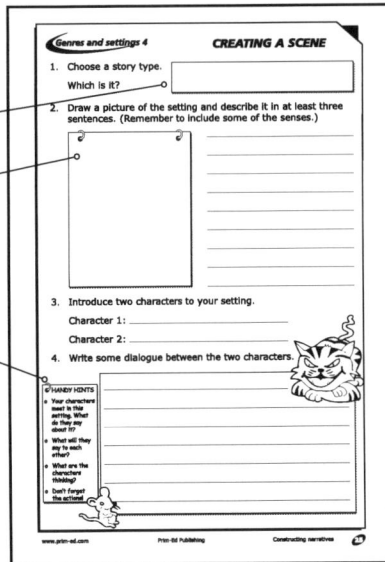

The generic pages provide the opportunity for each pupil to evaluate his/her efforts and gain a sense of achievement by earning a certificate of completion once his/her stories have been presented.

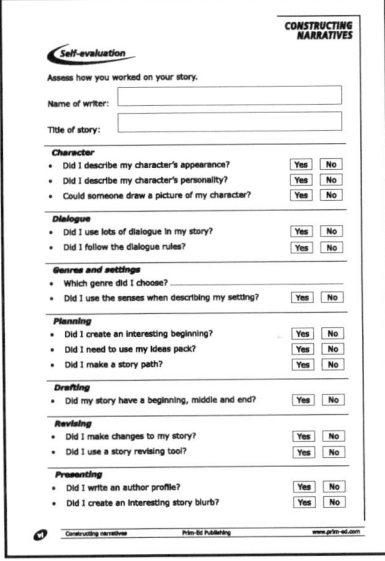

The **Self-evaluation** worksheet is to be given to the pupils once their stories are completed. Pupils may need to look back at their work and at their finished story to complete the evaluation. Remind them that all writers have areas that need improving and that it is important to be honest. Teachers can use this evaluation for assessment and reporting purposes.

This certificate can be presented to pupils who have satisfactorily completed the worksheets to the best of their ability. Teachers may wish to organise an assembly where pupils read their completed stories and are presented with the certificates.

Self-evaluation

Assess how you worked on your story.

Name of writer:

Title of story:

Character

- Did I describe my character's appearance?   Yes   No
- Did I describe my character's personality?   Yes   No
- Could someone draw a picture of my character?   Yes   No

Dialogue

- Did I use lots of dialogue in my story?   Yes   No
- Did I follow the dialogue rules?   Yes   No

Genres and settings

- Which genre did I choose? _____
- Did I use the senses when describing my setting?   Yes   No

---

Planning

- Did I create an interesting beginning?   Yes   No
- Did I need to use my ideas pack?   Yes   No
- Did I make a story path?   Yes   No

Drafting

- Did my story have a beginning, middle and end?   Yes   No

Revising

- Did I make changes to my story?   Yes   No
- Did I use a story revising tool?   Yes   No

Presenting

- Did I write an author profile?   Yes   No
- Did I create an interesting story blurb?   Yes   No

CREATIVE WRITING CERTIFICATE

Has successfully completed writing exercises on the following topics:

- Characters

- Dialogue

- Genres and settings

- Planning

- Drafting

- Revising

- Presenting

and has written an interesting and well-structured story titled

_____

Well done!

Signed: _____

Date: _____

The structure of each book in the series is identical, with the activities having the same headings and main focus. This allows pupils with different ability levels to be working on the same activity in the one classroom. The activities increase in difficulty throughout the levels of the books. This allows for easy use within a multi-ability classroom.

Country	Subject/Year	Objectives	Book 1	Book 2	Book 3
England	English (Writing) KS 2	*Composition* • choose form and content to suit a particular purpose	•	•	•
		• broaden vocabulary and use it in inventive ways	•	•	•
		• use language and style appropriate to the reader	•	•	•
		• use and adapt the features of a form of writing, drawing on reading	•	•	•
		• use features of layout, presentation and organisation effectively	•	•	•
		Planning and drafting • plan – note and develop initial ideas	•	•	•
		• draft – develop ideas from the plan into structured written text	•	•	•
		• revise – change and improve the draft	•	•	•
		• proofread – check the draft for spelling and punctuation errors	•	•	•
		• present – present a neat, correct and clear final copy	•	•	•
		• discuss and evaluate their own and other's writing	•	•	•
		Punctuation • use punctuation marks correctly in writing	•	•	•
		Spelling • check spelling using dictionaries	•	•	•
		Breadth of study • write to imagine and explore feelings and ideas, focusing on creative uses of language and how to interest the reader	•	•	•
		• write narratives	•	•	•
Northern Ireland	English (Writing) KS 2	*Planning* • plan written work through discussion with teacher and other pupils, gathering and organising ideas, preparing an outline and making notes	•	•	•
		Purpose • write for a variety of purposes, including to narrate and to express their thoughts, feelings and imaginings	•	•	•
		Context • write in response to a variety of experiences and contexts, including first-hand experience and in response to their reading	•	•	•
		Range • write in different forms and develop control over the different conventions demanded by these forms, including stories (based on personal experience and books read), creative and imaginative writing and dialogues	•	•	•
		• develop increasing competence in the use of punctuation	•	•	•
		• discuss various features of layout in texts they are reading	•	•	•
		• use knowledge of the alphabet to locate the correct spelling of words	•	•	•
		Expected outcomes • make expressive use of language when describing imaginings	•	•	•
		• observe the different conventions and structures demanded by the various forms of writing	•	•	•
		• locate the correct spelling of words that they need to use in writing through dictionaries	•	•	•
		• set out and punctuate direct speech	•	•	•
Republic of Ireland	English (Writing) 3rd/4th Class	*Receptiveness* • experience a classroom environment that encourages writing	•	•	
		• observe the teacher modelling different writing genres	•	•	
		• use personal reading as a stimulus to writing	•	•	
		• write stories that explore a variety of genres	•	•	
		Competence and confidence • write regularly and gradually extend the period of time over which a writing effort is sustained	•	•	
		• engage with the writing of one piece over a period of time	•	•	
		• learn to use questions as a mechanism for expanding and developing a story	•	•	
		• give sequence to ideas and events in stories	•	•	
		• learn to revise and redraft writing	•	•	
		• learn to use a wider range of punctuation marks with greater accuracy as part of the revision and editing process	•	•	
		Developing cognitive abilities • write in a variety of genres; e.g. stories	•	•	
		Emotional and imaginative • create stories	•	•	
		• write extended stories in book form	•		
	English (Writing) 5th/6th Class	*Receptiveness* • experience a classroom environment that encourages writing		•	•
		• experience interesting and relevant writing challenges		•	•
		• receive and give constructive responses to writing		•	•

Country	Subject/Year	Objectives	Book 1	Book 2	Book 3
	English (Writing) 5th/6th Class	*Competence and confidence* • write regularly and for a sustained length of time • engage in the writing of one piece over a period of time • observe the teacher improving writing – drafting, revising, editing • write independently through a process of drafting, revising, editing and publishing • observe the conventions of grammar, punctuation and spelling in his/her writing • use dictionaries to develop spelling • help others with editing their writing *Developing cognitive abilities* • write in a wide variety of genres; e.g. narratives • refine ideas and expression through drafting and redrafting *Emotional and imaginative* • write longer stories		• • • • • • • • • •	• • • • • • • • • •
Scotland	English (Writing) Level B	*Imaginative writing* • draft writing using questions and writing model • discuss first drafts of writing • be aware of aspects of stories from reading; e.g. plot, character, dialogue and setting *Punctuation and structure* • use capital letters and full stops correctly *Spelling* • after drafting, mark possible spelling errors and check correct spellings using a dictionary *Knowledge about language* • plan, draft and redraft during the writing process	• • • • • •		
	English (Writing) Level C	*Imaginative writing* • develop awareness of the importance of character, setting the scene and action *Punctuation and structure* • use commas correctly • use co-operative writing and discussion to reinforce the role of audience and motivate redrafting *Spelling* • after drafting, mark possible spelling errors and check correct spellings using a dictionary *Knowledge about language* • consider purpose and audience when considering what they plan to write or have written	• • • •	• • • • •	
	English (Writing) Level D	*Punctuation and structure* • look at texts to help learn about direct speech *Spelling* • use self-correction techniques to deal with spelling errors • use dictionaries to check spelling at the end of drafting		• • •	• • •
	English (Writing) Level E	*Imaginative writing* • draw on knowledge of what they have heard and read to use in own imaginative writing • develop characters and settings • show awareness of openings and resolutions • write, discuss and redraft sections of stories before putting them together to build longer, more fully-shaped works *Punctuation and structure* • check punctuation and organisation as part of the redrafting process • discuss drafting in pairs or small groups *Spelling* • use self-correction techniques to deal with spelling errors • use dictionaries to check spelling at the end of drafting			• • • • • • • •
Wales	English (Writing) KS 2	*Range* • write in response to a wide range of stimuli, including stories • use the characteristics of different kinds of writing • write in forms which include imaginative writing *Skills* • plan, draft and improve their work • discuss and evaluate their own and others' writing • plan – note and develop initial ideas • draft – develop ideas from the plan into structured written text • revise – alter and improve the draft • proofread – check the draft for spelling and punctuation errors • present – prepare a neat, correct and clear final copy • develop ability to organise and structure work in a variety of ways, using experience of fiction texts; e.g. a story with a beginning, middle and end • use punctuation marks correctly in writing • check spellings using dictionaries • use features of layout and presentation	• • • • • • • • • • • • • •	• • • • • • • • • • • • • •	• • • • • • • • • • • • • •

DRAWING CHARACTERS

Objective

- Uses pictures to represent ideas.

Teacher information

- Discuss the meaning of the word 'appearance'.

- Choose one pupil from the class and describe him/her in as much detail as possible. Record ideas on the board in point form.

- Discuss how pupils can turn this description into a picture, with particular emphasis on detail and colour.

- Read the description together.

- Identify points that describe the character's appearance.

- List the specific features that will need to be illustrated:
    - hair [long, blonde]
    - skin [pale]
    - eyes [blue]
    - height [tall]
    - dress [flowing silver gown]
    - wings [shimmering with stardust]

- Which features leave room for the illustrator's own choice?
    - hair [curly or straight]
    - other facial features [freckles? long nose?]
    - design on the gown?
    - wings [any pattern? colour of the stardust?]

    Include other suggestions from the class.

- Encourage the pupils to complete the worksheet individually. Remind them to include the given information, but suggest that they include some of their own choice ideas in their illustrations.

Additional activities

- Pupils share their completed worksheets with a partner and discuss the similarities and differences.

- Pupils produce a painting of Kira.

Assessment checklist

- Did the pupil understand the meaning of 'appearance' and participate in describing a friend in detail?

- Could the pupil identify specific features to be included in the worksheet illustration?

- Could the pupil suggest additional features?

- Did the final illustration contain a mixture of given and own choice features?

Characters 1

DRAWING CHARACTERS

When you read a story, you meet lots of different characters. The story tells you what each character looks like and all about his or her personality. While you are reading, you can imagine the character in your mind.

1. This is a description of a character called Kira. Read it carefully.

    'Kira is one of the stardust people. She lives on a bright and shining golden star. Kira has long blonde hair, pale skin and blue eyes. She is tall and wears a long flowing silver gown. Her wings always shimmer from being covered in stardust.'

2. Draw your picture of Kira in the box below. Use lots of colour and details.

DESCRIBING CHARACTERS

Objective

- Writes a basic description of a character.

Teacher information

- Brainstorm different types of characters; e.g. human, animal, fantasy. As a class, pupils choose a particular type; for example, a dragon.

- List things that will need to be described:
    - height
    - size
    - colour of skin and/or hair
    - facial features
    - age

Add other suggestions from the class.

- As a class, write three sentences to describe the character.

    For example: *'Ellegon was a baby dragon with bright green eyes and a wide grin. He was about as tall as a classroom desk. His body was covered with shining green scales and purple spots, but his wings shone a beautiful shade of gold.'*

- Read the worksheet together. Suggest pupils write their three sentences first and then draw a picture to match. Pupils complete their worksheet individually.

Additional activities

- Ask several pupils to read out their sentences. Discuss with the class what they would expect the picture to look like. Compare the answers with each pupil's actual drawing.

- In pairs, each pupil reads his/her descriptive sentences while a partner draws the character. Compare the two drawings. How different is the author's illustration from the partner's?

Assessment checklist

- Could the pupil list features to be described?
- Did the pupil participate in the class group activity?
- Was the pupil able to write three descriptive sentences?
- Did his/her picture match the written description?

DESCRIBING CHARACTERS

It's time to use your imagination! You are going to create a character of your own. Your character can be a person, an animal, a monster ... you choose!

1. What is your character's name?

2. Write three sentences about your character.

_____

_____

_____

_____

_____

3. Draw your character in the box below. Use lots of colour and detail.

CHARACTER PASSPORTS

Objective

- Describes selected characteristics of a character.

Teacher information

- Discuss the idea of a passport. What sort of information does a real passport have?

  If available, show the class an actual passport. Discuss:
  - photograph of the owner
  - full name
  - nationality
  - date and place of birth
  - whether the owner is male or female
  - when the passport was issued
  - when the passport will expire
  - signature of the owner
  - passport number
  - pages for stamps and visas from different countries

- Discuss the similarities and differences between a real passport and a character passport.

  Similarities: photo, name, age

  Differences: character passport lists mood, address, likes and dislikes.

- Choose a main character from a favourite classroom story. Complete a character passport for this character as a class.

  [Suggestions for stories: Roald Dahl characters, the Tashi series by Anna Fienberg, the Selby series by Duncan Ball.]

- Draw the pupils' attention to their created character from Characters 2, page 5. Pupils complete an individual passport for their created character.

Additional activities

- Pupils share their completed passports with the rest of the class.

- Design a front cover for the passport with a suitable crest; for example, a design that would match the character described, a book or even the school badge. Make the cover out of cardboard. Glue the character passport sheet inside and string a group of passports together for display.

Assessment checklist

- Could the pupil identify features of an actual passport?

- Could the pupil identify the similarities and differences between a real passport and a character passport?

- Did the pupil participate in the group creation of a character passport for a well-known character?

- Was the pupil able to create a passport for his/her own created character?

CHARACTER PASSPORTS

A passport has information about a person in it.

1. Complete this character passport for your character.

CHARACTER PASSPORT

Mood:

Happy ☐

Sad ☐

Angry ☐

Scared ☐

Likes: _____

_____

_____

Name: _____

Age: _____

Address: _____

_____

_____

Dislikes: _____

_____

_____

CREATING CHARACTERS

Objective

- Makes organisational decisions before writing.

Teacher information

- Discuss the difference between the two categories in the table: 'appearance' and 'personality'. Give some examples, such as:

  Appearance: age, height, hair, eye and skin colour, choice of clothes, facial features etc.

  Personality: are they friendly, shy, outgoing, cranky, sad, nervous? Do they have a particular like or dislike?

- Focus the pupil's attention on the previous two worksheets. Discuss how this information could be used for this activity.

Appearance

- Introduce the concept of writing in point form, rather than in complete sentences.

  - Use the example sentences about Ellegon the dragon from Characters 2:

    'Ellegon was a baby dragon with bright green eyes and a wide grin. He was about as tall as a classroom desk. His body was covered with shining green scales and purple spots, but his wings shone a beautiful shade of gold.'

  - Convert this description into point form:
    o baby dragon
    o bright green eyes, wide grin
    o tall as a classroom desk
    o shining green scales, purple spots, gold wings

- Pupils then look at their descriptive sentences for their own character and record these on the 'appearance' side of the worksheet.

Personality

- As a class, revise the character passport they created together for their chosen well-known character. Pupils use the information to complete the 'personality' side of the worksheet.

- Pupils then look at their individual character passports and use that information to complete the worksheet.

Additional activities

- Pupils introduce their completed character to the class.

- Pupils create a class display of their character worksheets. [This could be on the wall of the classroom or in a scrapbook, to create a source of different characters to be used in future story writing sessions.]

Assessment checklist

- Does the pupil understand the difference between appearance and personality?

- Did the pupil participate in whole-class activities?

- Did the pupil fill in each section of the worksheet for his/her individual character?

- Did the pupil use point form?

CREATING CHARACTERS

Choose a character you have already created or invent a new character. It can be a person, an animal, a monster or something else.

1. Complete the information about your character.

My character's name is:

This is what my character looks like.

Here are some interesting facts about my character's personality.

EFFECTIVE DIALOGUE

Objective

- Understands that dialogue is composed of different elements.

Teacher information

- Discuss the meaning of dialogue as words spoken or thought by characters in a story.

- Why should there be dialogue in a story?
  - Explain that dialogue gives readers lots of extra information— such as the way the characters speak and how they react to certain events.

- Discuss the idea that dialogue can make the story funnier or more exciting. It can also make the story easier and more interesting to read, because you want to know how the characters are going to react. If dialogue is badly written, the story can be confusing or boring—or both!

- Writing dialogue can be tricky. Remember to make sure:
  1. to choose words that match the age and personality of the characters
  2. the dialogue fits the mood and current events in the story.

- Good dialogue is made up of four things. These are:

  spoken words – show what the character is saying

  speech tags – show which character is speaking

  actions – show what the character is doing

  thoughts – show what the character is thinking or feeling

  These don't need to be included all at once, but there should be a balance of them throughout the story.

- Read the worksheet as a class group. Explain that the pupils are going to find the four parts of good dialogue by reading a short paragraph from a story.

- Complete this worksheet as a whole group. Pupils who show particular competence can move onto the additional activities and complete them independently.

Answers

'It was your fault!' **yelled Patrick**.

'No it wasn't! It was yours!' **Anne yelled back**.

(Patrick checked under the settee.) *'Stop whining and help me look'*, **he said**. *'Maybe Tick has crept back inside again.'*

'You weren't supposed to let her go outside', **said Anne**.

'I didn't!'

'Yes you did, you opened the door.'

'Well, how was I meant to know she wasn't sleeping on your lap any more? You should've been holding her.' (Patrick glared at his younger sister.) (Then Anne started to cry,) which made him feel even worse. What if a dog's got her or she's been hit by a car or something? **he thought**.

Additional activities

- Pupils can repeat the exercise by choosing a random section of dialogue from a favourite story. Alternatively, the class teacher can choose a particular section of dialogue to analyse from a shared reading session.

- Suggestions for stories to use:
  Stories by Roald Dahl
  Tashi series by Anna Fienberg
  Selby series by Duncan Ball

Assessment checklist

- Could the pupil suggest a definition for dialogue?
- Did the pupil participate in class discussion about the importance of dialogue?
- Could the pupil identify the four elements of dialogue?

EFFECTIVE DIALOGUE

In a story, the dialogue shows when characters are talking or thinking.

1. Good dialogue is made up of four parts. Read each part.

GOOD DIALOGUE

SPOKEN WORDS
Show what the character is saying.

SPEECH TAGS
Show which character is speaking.

ACTIONS
Show what the character is doing.

THOUGHTS
Show what the character is thinking or feeling.

2. In the following piece of dialogue:

- underline the spoken words
- put brackets around the actions
- highlight the speech tags
- put a box around the thoughts

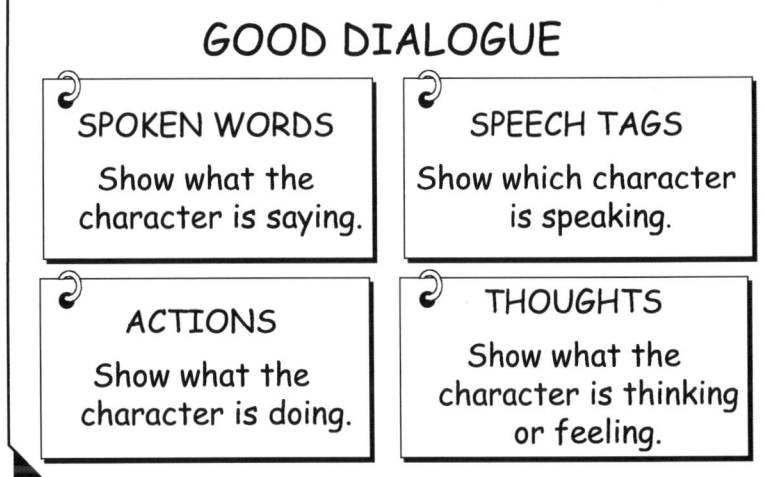

'It was **your** fault!' yelled Patrick.

'No it wasn't! It was **yours**!' Anne yelled back.

Patrick checked under the settee. 'Stop whining and help me look', he said. 'Maybe Tick has crept back inside again.'

'You weren't supposed to let her go outside', said Anne.

'I didn't!'

'Yes you did, you opened the door.'

'Well, how was I meant to know she wasn't sleeping on your lap any more? You should've been holding her.' Patrick glared at his younger sister. Then Anne started to cry, which made him feel even worse. What if a dog's got her or she's been hit by a car or something? he thought.

DIALOGUE RULES

Objective

- Writes dialogue correctly.

Teacher information

- How to set out dialogue correctly.

    1. Every time a new character speaks, you start a new paragraph.

        'Do you want to come over to my house this afternoon?' asked Sarah, as she and Mara sat down to eat their lunch.

        'OK, I'll ask my mum after school', answered Mara.

    2. Everything the character says out loud is put inside the speech marks.

        - If there is no speech tag, the full stop is also inside the speech marks.

            'I don't understand.'

        - If there is a speech tag, put a comma outside the speech marks and then add the speech tag.

            'I don't understand', said Kyle.

        - If there is a comma in what the character says, it goes inside the speech marks.

            'My cat is grey,' said Riley, 'but her kittens are black'.

    3. If the character speaks, does something and then speaks again, you don't need to take a new line for the second lot of speech.

        'I don't understand', said Kyle. He showed the homework to his dad. 'Can you please help me with question 4?'

    4. Speech marks are not necessary if a character is thinking something without speaking aloud.

        I can't believe it's so long until lunch, thought Ben. I'm hungry right now!

Answers

1. (a) Rule: 3   (b) Rule: 1   (c) Rule: 2(a)   (d) Rule: 4   (e) Rule: 2(b)
    (f) Rule: 2(c)

Additional activity

- Pupils can repeat the exercise by choosing a random piece of dialogue from a favourite story. Alternatively, the class teacher can choose a particular piece of dialogue to analyse from a shared reading session.

Assessment checklist

- Could the pupil match the dialogue examples to the correct rule?

DIALOGUE RULES

When writing dialogue, you must follow four important rules. These rules are:

1. *Every time a new character speaks, you start a new paragraph.*

2. *Everything the character says out loud is put inside the speech marks.*

   (a) *If there is no speech tag, the full stop is also inside the speech marks; for example, 'My cat is grey.'*

   (b) *If there is a speech tag, put a comma outside the speech marks and then add the speech tag; for example, 'My cat is grey', said Riley.*

   (c) *If there is a comma in what the character says, it goes inside the speech marks; for example, 'My cat is grey,' said Riley, 'but her kittens are black'.*

3. *If the character speaks, then does something and then speaks again, you don't need to take a new line for the second lot of speech.*

4. *Speech marks are not necessary if a character is thinking something without speaking aloud.*

1. Read the examples. Match them to the correct dialogue rule. Colour the number of the rule.

   (a) 'I don't understand', said Kyle. He showed the homework to his dad. 'Can you please help me with question 4?'

   | 1 | 2(a) | 2(b) | 2(c) | 3 | 4 |

   (b) 'Do you want to come over to my house this afternoon?' asked Sarah, as she and Mara sat down to eat their lunch.

   'OK, I'll ask my mum after school', answered Mara.

   | 1 | 2(a) | 2(b) | 2(c) | 3 | 4 |

   (c) 'I don't understand.'

   | 1 | 2(a) | 2(b) | 2(c) | 3 | 4 |

   (d) I can't believe it's so long until lunch, thought Ben. I'm hungry right now!

   | 1 | 2(a) | 2(b) | 2(c) | 3 | 4 |

   (e) 'I don't understand', said Kyle.

   | 1 | 2(a) | 2(b) | 2(c) | 3 | 4 |

   (f) 'My dog is grey,' said Jude, 'but her puppies are black'.

   | 1 | 2(a) | 2(b) | 2(c) | 3 | 4 |

DESIGNING DIALOGUE

Objective

- Uses direct speech.

Teacher information

- Review the rules of good dialogue, as well as the rules for setting out dialogue correctly.

- As a class, create a piece of dialogue as a group example.

  The teacher provides the first sentence and accepts pupil suggestions. The following is an example:

  'Wake up, sleepyhead!' said Dad, as he opened the door.

  'Is it morning already?' asked Sarah. She sat up in bed and rubbed her eyes. I wonder what's for breakfast, she thought.

  'Hurry up and get dressed', said Dad. 'If you take too long, your brother will eat all the pancakes.'

  'Pancakes!' Sarah jumped out of bed. 'Why didn't you say so?'

- Pupils are then encouraged to complete the worksheet individually.

Additional activities

- Pupils read their completed pieces of dialogue to each other.

- Repeat analysis of dialogue from Dialogue 2, using the pupils' dialogue as the example.

Assessment checklist

- Could the pupil remember the rules of good dialogue?

- Did the pupil create a short piece of dialogue incorporating these rules?

- Was the dialogue set out correctly?

DESIGNING DIALOGUE

You are going to write a short piece of dialogue between two characters.

1. Complete the information below to help you.

    *   Name of character 1:   *   Name of character 2:

        _____   _____

    *   Characters are talking about: _____

        _____

    *   Characters are:

        two friends   ☐   brother and sister   ☐

        mother and child   ☐   two neighbours   ☐

        teacher and pupil   ☐   _____   ☐

2. Write your dialogue below. Remember the four parts of good dialogue and to set your writing out correctly.

HANDY HINTS

o   Have you used speech tags?

o   Do the characters do things?

o   What are the characters thinking?

3. Share your dialogue with a friend. Can your friend see a way of improving your dialogue?

DEVELOPING DIALOGUE

Objective

- Writes a passage of increased complexity, using imaginative and correctly constructed dialogue.

Teacher information

- Review the piece of dialogue created as a group example.
- Brainstorm how this scene could be continued, by adding new characters and dialogue.

  Example of continued scene between Sarah and Dad (from page 14):

  Sarah's brother came out of the kitchen and headed for his room. 'Hi, Sarah!' he said. 'Too bad you missed breakfast.'

  'What do you mean, Ben?' asked Sarah, as she followed him down the hallway. 'Didn't you leave me any pancakes?'

  Their dad could hear them talking from the dining room. 'What's the matter?' he called out.

  'Ben's eaten all the pancakes!' said Sarah.

  'No, I haven't! I was just teasing!' called Ben. He poked out his tongue at Sarah, went into his room and closed the door.

  'Don't worry, Sarah,' said Dad, 'there are plenty left'.

  Brothers, thought Sarah as she walked quickly to the kitchen. I hope there's plenty of strawberry jam too!

- Pupils look at their own scene from the previous worksheet and think about how they could continue it. The teacher may need to do some individual conferencing to suggest ideas.
- Pupils complete the worksheet individually.

Additional activities

- Pupils share their completed pieces of dialogue with each other.
- Link with drama: Pupils act out their scene, using a narrator to read the actions and the speech tags.

Assessment checklist

- Did the pupil participate in the brainstorming session?
- Did the pupil continue his/her scene of dialogue?
- Was the dialogue set out correctly?

DEVELOPING DIALOGUE

Using the dialogue you wrote in Dialogue 3, you are going to introduce one more character and continue the conversation among the bigger group.

1. Complete the information below to help you.

   • Name of character 3: _____

   • Character 3 is a:

friend	☐	brother/sister	☐	neighbour	☐
teacher	☐	mum/dad	☐	_____	☐

   • Characters are talking about: _____

   _____

2. Write your dialogue below. Remember the four parts of good dialogue and to set your writing out correctly.

   HANDY HINTS

   o Who will join the characters next?

   o What will happen next?

   o Don't forget the actions!

   o What are the characters thinking?

3. Share your dialogue with a friend. How could you improve it?

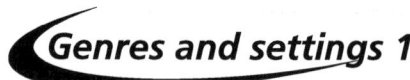

STORY GENRES

Objective

*   Understands conventions of particular text types.

Teacher information

*   Useful stories by genre

Family/School stories:	*James and the giant peach/The Twits* by Roald Dahl Hannah series by Libby Gleeson *Cabbage patch war* by Paul Jennings
Animal Stories:	Church Mice series by Graham Oakley Selby series by Duncan Ball *Fantastic Mr Fox* by Roald Dahl *The wind in the willows* by Kenneth Graeme
Mystery stories:	Emily Eyefinger series by Duncan Ball Famous Five and Secret Seven series by Enid Blyton
Action/Adventure:	Tashi series by Anna Fienberg
History stories:	Horrible Histories series (contains comic strips – graphic novel)
Science fiction and fantasy:	*The magic finger* by Roald Dahl The Enchanted Wood series by Enid Blyton

*   Brainstorm to find the titles of favourite class stories. List them on the board.

*   Read the definitions of story types as a class. Discuss which stories would match the story types.

*   Pupils then complete the worksheet individually, by choosing story titles that match the definition.

*   Pupils write their favourite story type in Question 2.

Additional activities

*   Pupils share their answers with each other. Discuss the concept that stories can often overlap between genres.

*   Collate the information from Question 2. Create a 'favourite story type' pictogram using the data.

Assessment checklist

*   Did the pupil participate in the class discussion regarding different story types?

*   Could the pupil identify an appropriate story type for the list of stories given?

*   Could the pupil identify an appropriate story type for stories of his/her own choice?

STORY GENRES

There are many different types (also called genres) of stories. Each type has its own set of rules to follow.

1. Read the definitions of the following story types. Can you think of an example of each type from the stories you have read? Write the name of the story or book in the box.

(a)	**Science fiction and fantasy:** In these stories, the characters live in a different world from the one we live in.	
(b)	**Historical fiction:** These stories are set in a specific time in the past.	
(c)	**Action/Adventure:** These stories are exciting and fast paced. Lots of different things happen to the characters. Just when you think the danger is over, something else happens!	
(d)	**Mystery:** The characters in these stories have a puzzle to solve. Along the way, the characters make mistakes and face danger. The ending is usually exciting!	
(e)	**Animal stories:** In these stories, animals are the important characters.	
(f)	**Family and school stories:** These stories happen in a family or school setting.	

2. Which is your favourite story type?

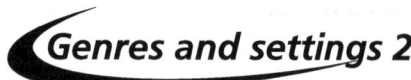
STORY SETTINGS

Objective

- Understands that writers need to set the scene clearly.

Teacher information

- Ask the class to list the five senses. Take the pupils on a 'senses walk' around the school. Instruct them to take notice of what they can see, hear, smell, touch or taste. On returning, discuss and list items for each sense. (Sight and sound will probably be the most popular. Encourage creative suggestions for the others.) Ask the pupils to create sentences that describe the school building in terms of the senses. Use the following focus questions:

  1. What did you see?
  2. What did you hear?
  3. What did you smell?
  4. What did you feel?
  5. What did you taste?

  (Not all senses need to be used, but the more that are used, the more descriptive the writing.)

- Discuss how many writers use the five senses when describing the settings in their stories. Explain to the class that the setting is where the story takes place; for example, in a forest, a school, in a park or on the moon.

- Read through the passage on the worksheet as a class. Complete the first two sentences together, then ask the pupils to complete the rest of the sheet individually.

Possible answers

2. (a) trees, rose bush, flowers, playground etc.

   (b) flowers

   (c) laughter of boys and girls

   (d) rough rope ladder

   (e) juicy crunchy apple

3. Teacher check

Additional activities

- Pupils compare their answers and share their pictures. Have all the details been included? How similar or different are the pictures?

- Pupils draw a picture of a different setting and write five sense sentences to match it.

Assessment checklist

- Could the pupil list the five senses?

- Did the pupil contribute to the class creation of a senses description?

- Could the pupil identify the senses within a given descriptive passage?

- Could the pupil draw an accurate picture of the setting described in the passage?

STORY SETTINGS

Once you have chosen the type of story you are going to write, you need to describe the setting. You can use the senses to make the setting more interesting.

1. Read the following passage.

> *Emma opened her eyes and found herself in a sunny park. There were lots of trees. Right behind her was a rosebush. Emma turned around to smell the beautiful flowers. In front of her was a huge playground with swings and slides and other things to play on. She heard the laughter of boys and girls playing, so she ran over to join them. She gripped the rough rope ladder and climbed up onto a platform that stood next to an apple tree full of ripe red apples. Emma reached out and picked one of the apples. She took a big bite. The apple was juicy and crunchy. Emma thought it was the best apple she had ever tasted.*

2. Finish these sentences :

   (a) Emma can see _____.

   (b) Emma can smell _____.

   (c) Emma can hear _____.

   (d) Emma can feel _____.

   (e) Emma can taste _____.

3. Draw a picture of the scene.

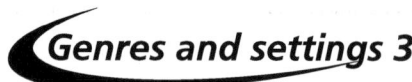

USING THE SENSES

Objective

•   Writes a detailed description of a scene or place.

Teacher information

•   Review the different story types from previous worksheets. What sorts of settings would match the particular genres?

•   Brainstorm a list of settings for each story type on the board.

     Example settings:

     Science fiction/Fantasy – space, the future, mountainous landscape, a different planet

     Family/School – modern-day house, school

     Animal – forest, jungle, farm

     Mystery – old building, deserted town, place with hidden trapdoors or secret pathways

     History – 50 years or earlier in any given country. (Remember to consider: how people travelled, what they wore, how they communicated etc.)

     Action/Adventure: airport, on board a train, bus, car – or any of the above settings.

•   As a class, pick one story type to work with. Create a description of the setting for the chosen story type, using as many of the senses as possible. Use adjectives to bring the story to life. Can the pupils imagine the setting in their minds?

•   Each pupil chooses a story type and a possible setting from the board to complete the worksheet.

Additional activities

•   Pupils share their descriptions and pictures.

•   Discuss the following questions, based on the shared work:

     1. How many pupils picked the same story type?

     2. How similar or different were their pictures?

     3. Which ones were the most effective? Why?

Assessment checklist

•   Could the pupil suggest appropriate settings for each story type?

•   Could the pupil write sentences to match their picture?

•   Could the pupil write five 'sense sentences'?

USING THE SENSES

1. Choose a story type.

   ☐ Science fiction and/or fantasy   ☐ Historical fiction

   ☐ Action/Adventure   ☐ Mystery

   ☐ Animal stories   ☐ Family and school stories

2. Draw a picture of the main setting.

3. Complete these sentences about your picture.

   This is a picture of _____.

   I can see _____.

   I can hear _____.

   I can smell _____.

   I can taste _____.

   I can feel _____.

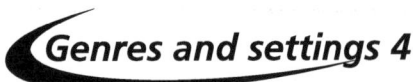
CREATING A SCENE

Objectives

- Writes a detailed description of a scene or place.
- Includes dialogue in the description.

Teacher information

- The aim of this worksheet is to start combining ideas so the pupils can begin to write a story. Pupils are going to introduce characters and dialogue into their setting.
- Read through the worksheet together. Explain the steps: describing a setting using the senses, introducing two characters and writing a short piece of dialogue.

    1. Review the list of story types and settings from previous worksheet.

       Encourage pupils to pick a totally different story type and complete the first part of the worksheet. This time, when writing their sense sentences, they do not have to start with: 'I can see, hear etc.'

    2. Review character creation and the correct use of dialogue.

       Suggest that one character is describing the scene, then meets the second character and they have a conversation. An opening sentence could be: *'Billy climbed the broad branches of the tall tree and looked down at the park below him ...'* [description continues]

- Pupils then complete the second half of the worksheet.

Additional activities

- Pupils share their work with the class.
- Discuss: Which is their favourite description from the two pieces of work? Why?
- Group pupils according to their chosen story type. Have them read their individual descriptions. How similar or different are the settings?

Assessment checklist

- Did the pupil's description use the five senses?
- Could the pupil recall elements of characterisation and dialogue?
- Could the pupil introduce two characters?
- Was the dialogue presented correctly?

CREATING A SCENE

1. Choose a story type.

    Which is it?

2. Draw a picture of the setting and describe it in at least three sentences. (Remember to include some of the senses.)

    _____

    _____

    _____

    _____

    _____

    _____

    _____

    _____

    _____

    _____

3. Introduce two characters to your setting.

    Character 1: _____

    Character 2: _____

4. Write some dialogue between the two characters.

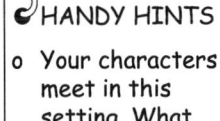

HANDY HINTS

o Your characters meet in this setting. What do they say about it?

o What will they say to each other?

o What are the characters thinking?

o Don't forget the actions!

    _____

    _____

    _____

    _____

    _____

    _____

STORY PLANS

Objective

- Understands and experiments with narrative structure—writing beginning sentences.

Teacher information

- Introduce the overall structure of a story. Remind the pupils that it is important to plan what is going to happen. There needs to be a *beginning* that captures the reader's attention; a *middle* that keeps the action going; and an effective, satisfying *ending*. The combination of all three forms the story's plot.

  The Beginning: The author needs to 'hook' his/her readers right from the start, so they will want to keep reading.

  The Middle: Keep the action going! Get the characters solving problems, but make sure that there is always something else they need to do. Build up to the biggest event or problem and leave a few clues along the way.

  The Ending: The characters solve the problem.

- Read the worksheet activity as a group. Discuss the idea that without a really effective beginning, the rest of the story may not be read.

- Encourage the pupils to follow the steps to complete the worksheet.

Additional activities

- Each pupil reads out his/her beginning sentence. Class vote: Which is the most interesting sounding story? (Voting can be by secret ballot if necessary.)

- Put all the beginning sentences into a hat and have each pupil draw one out. Following from the hook, the pupils write the next three sentences of the story.

Assessment checklist

- Did the pupil demonstrate an understanding of story structure?

- Did the pupil select a beginning sentence that he/she regarded as the most interesting?

- Did the pupil create three interesting beginning sentences of his/her own?

When writing a story, you need to hold your reader's attention right from the start.

1. Read the following four beginning sentences.

   (a) 'It was your fault!' yelled Patrick.

   (b) It was cold under the tree in the park.

   (c) Once upon a time, not so very long ago, there lived a young princess called Emma.

   (d) This is the story of three brothers named Ben, Bert and Will.

2. Which sentence do you think is the most interesting?

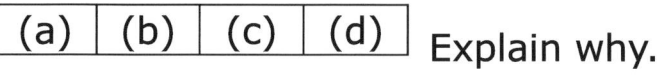 Explain why.

3. Write three of your own beginning sentences. Make them as interesting as you can.

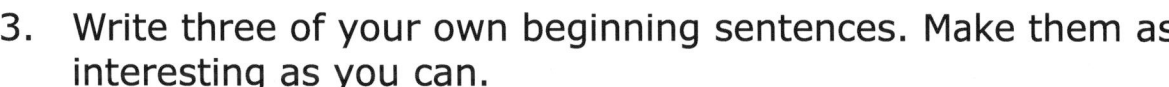

MAKING AN IDEAS PACK

Objective

- Creates an 'ideas' set of cards to use when writing creative stories.

Teacher information

- Read through the instructions with the class. On the board, brainstorm a list of items for each category.

- Pupils can use some of the brainstormed ideas from the board for each category or create their own ideas.

- Instruct pupils:

  – 'Who' set of cards: Write a different character onto each card; for example, a teacher, old lady, alien, mad scientist, pirate.

  – 'Where' set of cards: Write a different place onto each card; for example, shops, beach, jungle, city, space.

  – 'What' set of cards: Write a different object onto each card; for example, pen, book, spoon, map, wallet.

- Pupils may also wish to include a small picture on each card.

- Encourage the pupils to assemble their ideas packs, using as many of their own ideas as possible.

- After completion, cut out each card and shuffle each separate pile. Lay them out in order; for example, 'old lady, 'shop', 'book'.

- It is important that the pupil retains his/her cards for further activities.

- Look at the cards selected. Review the steps for writing an interesting beginning sentence, or 'hook', from page 27. Create a story beginning as a class; for example, *'Grandma Williams stared at the book in the window of the secondhand bookshop.'*

- With their complete ideas packs, pupils select their own cards and write an interesting beginning sentence to match the cards, on a separate sheet of paper.

- Teachers may wish to collect all of the pupils' cards and laminate them. The cards could be placed in separate 'who', 'what' and 'where' boxes and be made available to the pupils during creative writing.

Additional activities

- Pupils share their 'hooks' with each other.
- Pupils swap the cards with a friend and write a 'hook' for their friend's cards.

Assessment checklist

- Did the pupil contribute to the brainstorming list?
- Did the pupil create an ideas pack?
- Could the pupil use his/her ideas pack to create a sentence beginning?

MAKING AN IDEAS PACK

Sometimes when you have to write a story, your mind can go blank. Using an 'ideas' set of cards can help you. Complete your cards by writing an idea and drawing a picture on each.

Who	What	Where

Who	What	Where

Who	What	Where

Who	What	Where

THE STORY PATH

Objective

- Uses planning and reviewing strategies to plan a story.

Teacher information

- As a class, review the chosen cards from the ideas pack and create the beginning of a story.

  For example, *Beginning: An old lady looks into the window of a shop and sees a book she likes.*

- Revise the concept of the structure of a story from page 26. What could happen next? Remind the pupils that some problems will need to occur. Ask some questions to get the discussion going:

  1. What is so special about the book?

  2. What if the shop owner says it isn't for sale?

  3. How could she try to get the book?

  Record suggestions on the board. Then ask:

  'How can we solve the problem and end the story?'

  Once again, record suggestions on the board.

- Read through the steps on the story path.

- As a group, create a story path for this story. What needs to go in each step?

Possible answers

1. A description of the old lady.

2. To get the book.

3. Things she does to try to get the book.

4. The solution to the problem.

   Discuss the idea that each step needs more detail and that each pupil may have different descriptions and ideas.

- Pupils complete the activity, making any changes they like to the group story path.

Additional activities

- Pupils share their ideas.

- Using large sheets of paper, paint a story path for display in the classroom.

- Display individual worksheets of completed story paths.

- Pupils write the story using the information on the worksheet.

Assessment checklist

- Could the pupil recall the structure of a story?

- Could the pupil suggest answers for each step?

- Did the pupil complete the story path, adding details when necessary?

THE STORY PATH

These ideas cards have been chosen.

Who

Where

What

This is the story beginning.

An old lady looks into the window of a shop and sees a book she likes.

In your group, make a path for your story to follow.
Discuss each part then write your ideas on the 'stones'.

HANDY HINTS
o What is so special about the book?
o What if the shop owner says it isn't for sale?
o How could she try to get the book?

1. Describe your character.

2. What does your character want to do?

3. What problem(s) does your character want to solve?

4. How does your character solve the problem(s)?

PATH OF IDEAS

Objective

- Selects one or more planning strategies to create a structured narrative.

Teacher information

- Explain to the pupils that this is an individual activity, which follows from the previous whole-class activity on page 31. The steps completed will be the same, except that they will be completed by pupils individually, rather than as a class.

- Each pupil selects the required cards from his/her own ideas pack.

- Each pupil creates a story path for the selected cards, adding detail to steps as necessary.

- Instruct the pupils to create a story structure first, using the 'who', 'what' and 'where' cards for the story beginning.

  The teacher may need to do some individual conferencing to suggest ideas for the middle and end of the pupils' stories. Asking 'what if' questions is helpful here.

Additional activities

- Pupils share their completed work.
- Display completed story paths.

Idea for display

- Paint a large 'footpath' with individual stepping stones onto large sheets of paper and hang them from the back wall of the classroom. Each pupil copies his/her story structure onto an individual 'stone'.

Assessment checklist

- Did the pupil use the ideas pack correctly?
- Did the pupil create a story path, adding detail when necessary?

PATH OF IDEAS

1. Choose three 'ideas' cards. Record the cards you chose.

    Who: _____

    Where: _____

    What: _____

2. Write a story beginning—just one sentence that will 'hook' the reader into your story.

3. Complete the story path.

1. Describe your character.

2. What does your character want to do?

3. What problem(s) does your character want to solve?

4. How does your character solve the problem(s)?

BEGINNING A STORY

Objective

- Drafts the beginning of an imaginary story.

Teacher information

- Explain to the pupils that they are going to use all the things they have learnt so far to create a complete story.

  (Pupils can use the story from their story path, as it is already planned, as opposed to starting a new story.)

- What should the beginning of the story do?
  - introduce the characters
  - introduce the setting
  - show what the characters are doing

- Encourage the pupils to use the page for free writing. They will be able to edit and revise later, but for now should concentrate on getting the story written down.

- Pupils focus on the beginning of the story and complete the worksheet. (Extra copies of the worksheet may be needed for very keen writers!)

- Teacher to act as facilitator, providing suggestions as needed.

- Pupils share their story beginning with a partner and discuss how it could be improved.

Additional activities

- Pupils share their work with the group.

- Pupils could provide some illustrations for the story so far, to be included for presentation and/or display.

Assessment checklist

- Did the pupil follow the story plan to begin the story?

- Did the story begin with an interesting sentence?

- Were characters and settings introduced?

BEGINNING A STORY

1. Write the beginning of your story. It should describe your main characters and what they are doing. It should also describe the setting.

HANDY HINTS

o Look at your story path. Use Steps 1 and 2.

o Remember, your first sentence has to 'hook' the reader.

o Introduce the characters in your story.

o Introduce the setting.

o Show what the characters are doing.

2. Ask a friend to read your story beginning. How could it be improved?

CONTINUING A STORY

Objective

- Drafts the middle of an imaginative story with a definite storyline.

Teacher information

- Explain to the class that they will now draft the middle of their story.

- Ask the pupils to reread the beginning of their story. The purpose of rereading is to get a clear idea of where the story is up to. Pupils should not be concerned with editing at this stage.

- Review the structure of a story. What needs to happen in the middle of a story?

    - continue the events

    - problems need to appear for the characters to solve

    - the middle should end with the introduction of the biggest problem in the story; this will be the most dramatic part.

- Pupils continue their story on the worksheet. Remind them to use Step 3 of their story plan.

Additional activities

- Pupils share their work with the group.

- Pupils could provide some illustrations for the middle of the story, to be included for presentation and/or display.

Assessment checklist

- Could the pupil recall the elements of the middle of a story?

- Did this section of the story flow on from the beginning section?

- Did the pupil continue to follow the story path?

- Does this section end at the most dramatic point?

CONTINUING A STORY

1. Read your story beginning again.

2. Write the middle of your story. It should carry on from the beginning. In the middle of your story, there should be a big problem for your characters to solve.

HANDY HINTS

o Look at Step 3 of your story path.

o What are your characters doing?

o What is the problem in your story?

o Is there any dialogue in your story?

3. Ask a friend to read your story middle. How could it be improved?

ENDING A STORY

Objective

- Drafts the end of an imaginative story with a definite storyline in which some events are clearly related to the resolution of a problem.

Teacher information

- Explain to the class that they will now complete their story.

- Ask pupils to reread the two sections of their story for content rather than correction.

- Discuss the ending of the story. What needs to happen in this section?
  - the big problem needs to be solved
  - the loose ends have to be tied up

- Discuss the fact that not all endings are happy. It is OK to have a sad ending, as long as everything has been resolved and the story makes sense to the reader.

- Pupils complete their individual story. Remind them to use the final step from their story plan.

- Teacher provides suggestions if necessary.

Additional activities

- Pupils share their work with the group.

- Pupils could provide some illustrations for the final section of the story, to be included for presentation and/or display.

Assessment checklist

- Did the pupil reread his/her story for content?

- Was the pupil able to contribute to the discussion about the ending of a story?

- Did the pupil's ending resolve the biggest problem in the story in an effective way?

ENDING A STORY

1. You will now write the end of your story. The main problem in your story should be solved.

HANDY HINTS

o Look at Step 4 of your story path.

o What is the big problem in your story?

o How will the big problem be solved?

o Is there dialogue in your story?

o Is there a hero in your story?

o Have all the 'loose ends' been tied up?

2. Ask a friend to read your story ending. How could it be improved?

COVER IT

Objective

- Considers the presentation of book covers with regard to their impact on the reader.

Teacher information

- Display a number of front covers of collections of short stories and picture books.

  Depending on the time of the year, this lesson could link with 'Book Week' activities.

- What things make the cover effective?

  – discuss the use of colour and design

- What things are always included on a front cover?

  Title of story

  Name of author

  Name of illustrator

  Name of publisher

- Pupils complete worksheet individually.

Additional activities

- Linking with art and design: Pupils use a medium of their own choice to create their front cover; e.g. paint, photography, computer graphics.

- Display the completed front covers in the classroom.

Assessment checklist

- Did the pupil participate in the discussion of effective book covers?
- Could the pupil identify the common elements of a book cover?
- Did the pupil design an effective book cover for his/her own story?

COVER IT

1. Look at the front cover of your favourite book. What do you like about it?

2. Invent a title for your imaginary story.

3. Design the front cover. Don't forget to include a colourful picture and your name as the author and illustrator.

PRACTISING REVISING

Objective

- Experiments with strategies for proofreading text and his/her own writing.

Teacher information

- Explain to the class that they will be reading text that needs to be revised. If available, copy the text onto an overhead transparency so that Questions 1 and 2 can be completed as a whole class.

- Read the text together once. Read Question 2 and explain that the aim is to find the mistakes in the text.

- As you read the text again, ask pupils to tell you when they see an error. Mark the errors and corrections on the board. The pupils then copy these corrections onto their own worksheet.

- Let the class know that they have been 'editing' or 'revising' the story. Revising is one of the most important stages of writing. No author writes a perfect story on the first draft.

- Making revision beads

  Materials per pupil:
  - five hollow beads
  - wool or string

  Note: Have a needle available for threading the beads, for pupils who may find this task difficult.

- Pupils make their revision beads. These beads can be used whenever a piece of writing needs improving. Each time an error is found or a phrase/sentence is improved, the pupils will move a bead across.

- Pupils keep their revision beads with them during literacy lessons. The beads will encourage the pupils to check their writing before they announce that they are finished.

Answers 2

Suddenly, something very strange happened▪ As Emma looked in the mirror, a little girl appeared. She had <u>brown</u> hair, blue eyes, <u>lots</u> of freckles and a big friendly smile.

*'Hello, Emma', she said. 'My name is **K**atherine. Do you want to come and play with me?'*

Emma just <u>stared</u> at her. 'How did you get in there?' she asked▪

*Katherine smiled. 'That's a <u>special</u> magic secret. **C**ome on! Come and play!'*

Additional activity

- Pupils can make different revision tools, using different materials.

Assessment checklist

- Did the pupil follow the instructions to create a story revision tool?

- Could the pupil find the spelling mistakes in the text?

- Could the pupil find the missing full stops in the text?

- Could the pupil highlight the two letters that should be capital letters in the text?

- Could the pupil use a dictionary to find the correct spelling of the misspelt words?

  For more activities that develop and improve revision skills, see: 'Proofreading and Editing Skills' by Prim-Ed Publishing.

PRACTISING REVISING

1. Read the text

> *Suddenly, something very strange happened As Emma looked in the mirror, a little girl appeared. She had browne hair, blue eyes, lotts of freckles and a big friendly smile. 'Hello, Emma', she said. 'My name is katherine. Do you want to come and play with me?' Emma just starred at her. 'How did you get in there?' she asked Katherine smiled. 'That's a speshel magic secret. come on! Come and play!'*

2. • Underline the four spelling mistakes. Write the correct spelling above the words.

    • Find the two missing full stops. Write them in.

    • Highlight the two letters that should be capital letters.

3. Making revision beads

    You will need:

    –   five beads with holes in them

    –   wool or string

    What to do:

    1. Thread the wool through your beads. Tie a knot at each end.

    2. Place your beads in front of you when you are revising.

    3. When you find a mistake, move one bead to the opposite end of the string.

    4. Keep reading and looking for mistakes until all the beads have been moved.

    5. If you are happy with your work—stop! If not, keep revising by moving the beads back and starting again.

REVISING THE BEGINNING

Objectives

- Experiments with strategies for proofreading his/her own writing.
- Presents a revised version of a story beginning.

Teacher information

- Pupils need to have completed activity:

  'Drafting – 1: Beginning a story' (page 35) prior to this activity.

- Pupils require a red, green and blue pencil to complete the activity.

- Once the pupils have completed their stories, introduce the editing stage. Explain to the class that they will now revise their story. Revising is one of the most important stages of writing. No author writes a perfect story on the first draft.

- Pupils will need a copy of the beginning of their story with them ('Beginning a story' – page 35). Explain to the class that they will only be revising the beginning part of their story in this lesson. This may only be one or two paragraphs. A whole lesson has been allocated for this so pupils will have time not only to find mistakes, but to improve their story if required.

- Discuss the concept that it is a good idea to take a break in between finishing the story and starting to revise it. It is easier to find mistakes and text that needs improving after leaving the writing for a while. (Teachers may wish to start the revision stage on a Monday.)

- Explain to the class what is required at each step of the worksheet. Encourage pupils to read aloud to see if their writing sounds correct. Pupils may work in pairs and ask their partner if they think their writing sounds correct and if their story is interesting. Remind pupils to make the corrections onto their draft worksheet.

- Remind pupils that they have completed activities that should help them to create an effective story beginning. Pupils can look at previous activities, such as:

  - 'Describing characters' (Page 5) – 'Dialogue rules' (Page 13)
  - 'Creating a scene' (Page 25) – 'Story plan' (Page 27)

- Pupils proofread and edit the beginning of their story. They write the revised version onto the worksheet—using the back of the sheet if necessary.

Additional activities

- Pupils can use their revision tools created in the previous activity ('Practising revising' – page 43) to record the number of improvements made.

- Pupils keep a dictionary of misspelt words that they can include in their weekly spelling lists.

Assessment checklist

- Did the pupil mark corrections onto his/her own first draft?
- Did the pupil use a dictionary to correct spelling errors?
- Did the pupil read his/her work aloud—either to himself/herself or to a partner?
- Did the pupil present/publish the edited version onto the worksheet?
- Did the pupil use a revision tool?

REVISING THE BEGINNING

Revising is a very important part of writing. No-one can write a perfect story on the first draft!

1. Reread the beginning of your story.

2. Edit your story using a red, green and blue pencil.

    (a) Circle with a red pencil any words you think are misspelt. Use a dictionary to check them and write the correct spelling.

    (b) Add the missing punctuation with a blue pencil. Look for missing full stops, capital letters and commas.

    (c) Check your dialogue. If you haven't started a new line every time a character speaks, draw a star (*) using your green pencil.

3. Does your story beginning:

• 'hook' the reader with an exciting first sentence?	Yes	No
• describe the setting?	Yes	No
• introduce the characters?	Yes	No

    If you answered 'no', rewrite parts of your beginning.

4. Present the corrected beginning of your story below.

    _____
    _____
    _____
    _____
    _____
    _____
    _____
    _____

REVISING THE MIDDLE

Objectives:

- Experiments with strategies for proofreading his/her own writing.
- Presents a revised version of the middle of his/her own story.

Teacher information

- Pupils need to have completed activity:

  'Drafting – 2: Continuing a story' (page 37) prior to this activity.

- Pupils require a red, green and blue pencil to complete the activity.

- Explain to the class that they will now revise the middle of their story. Revising is one of the most important stages of writing. No author writes a perfect story on the first draft.

- Pupils will need a copy of the middle of their story with them ('Continuing a story' – page 37). Explain to the class that they will only be revising the middle part of their story in this lesson. This may only be one or two paragraphs. A whole lesson has been allocated for this so pupils will have time to not only find mistakes, but to improve their story if required.

- Explain to the class what is required at each step of the worksheet. Encourage pupils to read aloud to see if their writing sounds correct. Pupils may work in pairs and ask their partner if they think their writing sounds correct and if their story is interesting. Remind pupils to make the corrections onto their draft worksheet.

- Remind pupils that they have completed activities that should help them to create an effective story middle. Pupils can look at previous activities, such as:

  - 'Effective dialogue' (Page 11)
  - 'Dialogue rules'   (Page 13)
  - 'Path of ideas'   (Page 33)

- Pupils proofread and edit the middle of their story. They write the revised version onto the worksheet—using the back of the sheet if necessary.

Additional activities

- Pupils can use their revision tools created in the previous activity ('Practising revising' – page 43) to record the number of improvements made.

- Pupils keep a dictionary of misspelt words that they can include in their weekly spelling lists.

Assessment checklist

- Did the pupil mark corrections onto his/her own first draft?
- Did the pupil use a dictionary to correct spelling errors?
- Did the pupil read his/her work aloud—either to himself/herself or to a partner?
- Did the pupil present/publish the edited version onto the worksheet?
- Did the pupil use a revision tool?

REVISING THE MIDDLE

Revising is a very important part of writing. No-one can write a perfect story on the first draft!

1. Reread the middle part of your story.

2. Edit your story using a red, green and blue pencil.

   • Circle with a red pencil any words you think are misspelt. Use a dictionary to check them and write the correct spelling.

   • Add the missing punctuation with a blue pencil. Look for missing full stops, capital letters and commas.

   • Check your dialogue. If you haven't started a new line every time a character speaks, draw a star (*) using your green pencil.

3. | | |
   |---|---|
   | (a) Does the middle of your story have action? | Yes / No |
   | (b) Is there a problem for the characters to solve? | Yes / No |

   If you answered 'no', rewrite parts of the middle of your story.

4. Present the corrected middle of your story below. (Continue on the back.)

_____

_____

_____

_____

_____

_____

_____

_____

_____

_____

REVISING THE END

Objectives:

- Experiments with strategies for proofreading his/her own writing.
- Presents a revised version of the end of his/her own story.

Teacher information

- Pupils need to have completed activity:

  'Drafting – 3: Ending a story' (page 39) prior to this activity.

- Pupils require a red, green and blue pencil to complete the activity.

- Explain to the class that they will now revise the end of their story. Revising is one of the most important stages of writing. No author writes a perfect story on the first draft.

- Pupils will need a copy of the end of their story with them ('Ending a story' – page 39). Explain to the class that they will only be revising the end of their story in this lesson. This may only be one or two paragraphs. A whole lesson has been allocated for this so pupils will have time to not only find mistakes, but to improve their story if required.

- Explain to the class what is required at each step of the worksheet. Encourage pupils to read aloud to see if their writing sounds correct. Pupils may work in pairs and ask their partner if they think their writing sounds correct and if their story is interesting. Remind pupils to make the corrections onto their draft worksheet.

- Remind pupils that they have completed activities that should help them to create an effective story ending. Pupils can look at previous activities, such as:

  – 'Effective dialogue' (Page 11)
  – 'Dialogue rules'   (Page 13)
  – 'Path of ideas'   (Page 33)

- Pupils proofread and edit the end of their story. They write the revised version onto the worksheet—using the back of the sheet if necessary.

Additional activities

- Pupils can use their revision tools created in the previous activity ('Practising revising' – page 43) to record the number of improvements made.

- Pupils keep a dictionary of misspelt words that they can include in their weekly spelling lists.

Assessment checklist

- Did the pupil mark corrections onto his/her own first draft?
- Did the pupil use a dictionary to correct spelling errors?
- Did the pupil read his/her work aloud—either to himself/herself or to a partner?
- Did the pupil present/publish the edited version onto the worksheet?
- Did the pupil use a revision tool?

REVISING THE END

Revising is a very important part of writing. No-one can write a perfect story on the first draft!

1. Reread the end of your story.

2. Edit your story using a red, green and blue pencil.

   • Circle with a red pencil any words you think are misspelt. Use a dictionary to check them and write the correct spelling.

   • Add the missing punctuation with a blue pencil. Look for missing full stops, capital letters and commas.

   • Check your dialogue. If you haven't started a new line every time a character speaks, draw a star (*) using your green pencil.

3. (a) Do the characters solve the problem?   Yes   No

   (b) Have all of the questions been answered?   Yes   No

   If you answered 'no', rewrite parts of the end of your story.

4. Present the corrected end of your story below.

_____

_____

_____

_____

_____

_____

_____

_____

_____

_____

_____

AUTHOR PROFILE

Objective

- Creates a short passage of writing for a specific purpose.

Teacher information

- Have available a selection of books that contain author profiles with photographs.
- Ask the pupils to bring in their favourite book for this lesson.
- Show the pupils where an author profile is generally found.
- Share the profiles with the class. Discuss the information contained in an author profile.
  - personal information about the author
  - information about other stories he/she has written
  - sometimes a photograph
- Ask the pupils to choose their favourite author. Brainstorm to discover information that they already know and discuss where they could find other facts.
- Suggestions for authors to research:
  - Allan Ahlberg
  - Babette Cole
  - Roald Dahl
  - Dick King Smith
  - Martin Waddell
- Use the Internet or library to research information about the authors.
- A number of the above authors have their own websites.
- Search for authors under specific publishing houses; e.g. Penguin, Scholastic.

  A good general website for author information is:

  http://www.ukchildrensbooks.co.uk
- Pupils complete the worksheet for their chosen author.

Additional activities

- Pupils can complete a fact file about their author and present it to the class.
- Display the author profiles in the classroom.

Assessment checklist

- Could the pupil identify the author profile in his/her chosen story?
- Could the pupil identify the type of information found in an author profile?
- Did the pupil complete a profile for a favourite author?

AUTHOR PROFILE

An author profile is usually found on the inside back cover of a book. It contains interesting information about the author and sometimes has a photo.

1. Think of your favourite author. Find out five interesting facts about him or her and complete the author profile.

   Author's name: _____

2. Draw or glue a picture of your author in the box.

HANDY HINTS

o Where was the author born?

o What books has the author written?

o What types of books does the author write?

INTRODUCING YOU

Objective

- Selects subject matter and language to suit a specific audience and purpose.

Teacher information

- Encourage the pupils to reread the profile on their favourite author. Revise the different types of information included in a profile.

- Explain to the pupils that they are going to create an author profile about themselves. Brainstorm the information that they might like to include.
  - their name
  - city/town/village where they live
  - members of their family
  - hobbies
  - stories that they have written or would like to write
  - photograph of themselves

- Pupils complete the worksheet individually.

- Pupils draw a picture or attach a photo of themselves in the box.

Additional activities

- In pairs, pupils swap profiles and introduce each other.
- Display completed profiles around the classroom.

Assessment checklist

- Did the pupil recall the information needed in an author profile?
- Did the pupil create his/her own author profile, including this information?

Imagine you are a famous author!

1. Think of five interesting facts about yourself and complete the profile. Pretend you are someone else writing about you. Use 'he/she' instead of 'I'.

2. Add a photo or draw a picture of yourself.

    Author's name: _____

HANDY HINTS

o Where was he/she born and where does he/she live now?

o What stories has the author written?

o What type of stories does he/she like to write?

o Where does the author go to school?

o What does the author do in his/her spare time?

STORY BLURBS

Objective

- Examines how writers try to engage audiences.

Teacher information

- Using a variety of picture and story books, read the blurbs from the back cover of each to the class. Explain that a blurb is a short paragraph about the story, designed to make the reader want to buy the book. Discuss the type of information that is included in each of the chosen blurbs, as well as the information that is left out. Which blurb is the most effective?

  IN: characters in the story

           events from the story

           hints at the action to come

  OUT: the actual ending!

- Pupils choose one blurb, from either the examples provided or from a book of their own choice, and complete the worksheet.

Additional activity

- The pupils choose a blurb that doesn't appeal to them and rewrite it so that it sounds more interesting.

Assessment checklist

- Could the pupil identify the elements of a story blurb?

- Could the pupil nominate the most effective blurb and provide a reason for his/her choice?

- Could the pupil complete an analysis of a chosen blurb? [Worksheet activity]

STORY BLURBS

A blurb is generally found on the back cover of a book. It is written to make the reader want to buy the book.

1. Choose a book and read its blurb.

2. Answer the following questions about the story blurb.

(a) Title of the book:

(b) Author:

(c) Who is the story about?

(d) What is happening in the story?

(e) Does this story sound interesting to you? Yes No

Explain why.

(f) Would you buy this book? Yes No

INTRODUCING YOUR STORY

Objective

- Examines how writers try to engage audiences and experiments with these techniques.

Teacher information

- Review the information included in a story blurb.

- Explain to the pupils that they are each going to write a blurb for the story they have written.

- Remind them that they are trying to convince someone to read their story. What information should they include?

  - names of characters

  - a brief summary of some of the events

  - hints at what is to come, without giving away the ending

- As a group, write a blurb for a well-known nursery rhyme or folktale.

  Example: *'Little Red Riding Hood's grandmother isn't feeling well, so Red decides to take her a basket of goodies. When she gets to her grandmother's house, things start to feel strange. Her grandmother's voice sounds funny, she has huge teeth and she seems to have lots more hair than usual. Is it really Grandma – or is Little Red Riding Hood in danger?'*

- Pupils complete the worksheet for their own story. Pupils will need to reread their story created during previous lessons.

Additional activity

- Pupils read their blurbs aloud to the group. The class can vote on which blurb sounds the most interesting and why.

Assessment checklist

- Did the pupil participate in the creation of a group story blurb?
- Did the pupil's created blurb contain the correct elements?

INTRODUCING YOUR STORY

1. Read a story you have written. Write a blurb for your story. Make it as interesting as you can, so that people will want to read your story. Make sure you don't give away the ending!

_____

_____

_____

_____

_____

_____

_____

_____

_____

_____

_____

_____

_____

_____

_____

_____

_____

_____

HANDY HINTS

o Name your characters!

o Retell part of your story!

o Include the setting.

o Explain the problem that needs to be solved.

o You can have some exciting dialogue in your blurb.

o Don't give away the ending!